The Proposition

Marianna Albert

I dedicate this book to my grandma, Margaret Piccolo.
Heaven is lucky to have you.

ACKNOWLEDGMENTS

Here they are very quickly.

Carmela Romero, Heather Kabashi, Angela Albert, and Juliann Merchant, thank you for reading and editing.

I can never forget my children, Aaron, Kayla, Rylee, and Jason. Always stay young at heart.

Last but not least my husband, Bobby, perfect should be your middle name.

~

It was a cool October night. I was in my room trying to figure out how I was going to make a decision that would change not only my life, but the life of my girlfriend. I've been dating Charlie since I was a junior in high school. We had an unbelievably great relationship; everything was perfect from the way we spoke to each other to how we laid in bed. Tonight I had to break up with her. I just don't know how I'm going to do it. I made this decision when I decided to become a lawyer. The first two years of college was a breeze and Charlie was there the whole time with me. I always did well in school without much effort. Now I had to buckle down if I want to go to law school. I never want to hurt Charlie. I really love her, but it will never work out, and I'm sure once I explain everything to her she'll understand.

I stood up, looked at myself in the mirror, and pushed my hands through my reddish brown hair. I took a few deep breaths. "Come on Jay. You can do this," I said to my Prince Harry reflection in the mirror.

Ever since middle school, all my teachers said how much I looked like Prince Harry. Imagine me, the *Prince of Wales*. I know I have his hair and eye color. Charlie always used to say when I smile my eyes scrunch up like his do. I'm tall at 6'2, and I have a lean, but fit body; I usually go to the gym at least five times a week. I glanced at my phone which I had casually thrown on my bed. I walked over and entered in my code. I scrolled down until I saw Charlie's name and stared at it for the next ten minutes. Why am I having such a hard time with this? I had gone over it multiple times in my head. I just have to do it.

I pressed her number and the phone started ringing. I knew she would be getting ready to go out for her best friend, Marisa's 21st birthday, and I knew my words would destroy her night.

She picked up the phone on the second ring and blared into the phone, "I'm almost ready!"

"It's not Marisa."

"Oh, hi Jay. What's going on? I'm just about to meet Marisa."

"Charlie, I think I need some space from you."

"Jay, what did you say?"

Those were the last words I heard her say as I hung up. It didn't go exactly as planned. I wanted to explain the reasons why I was breaking up with her. She deserved an explanation. I just couldn't get it out. I did it the fast and easy way. She'll get over me. Eventually.

I laid on my bed and thought about what I had done for the next half hour. I sat up and decided she'd get over me. I walked over to my closet opened the door and bent down. The floor boards creaked from the numerous times I bent down in this same exact place. I traced my fingers along the floor and popped the board out. I put my hand in the hole and pulled out a bottle of pills. I read the bottle. Jason Bushnell, take two pills, one in the morning and one at night. This medication may cause dizziness and drowsiness.

I opened the bottle and shook out a pill. I stared at the pill for a few minutes, put it back in the bottle, and decided I didn't need it right now. I can do this. I lived without them for the last three years. I stood up, slammed the closet door shut, leaned up against it, and thought of Charlie. She'll get over me, eventually, I hoped.

I had already made plans to go out tonight. I was going to hang out with a few friends from college. We were meeting at a local bar. I took a cab to the bar because I already knew I would be too drunk to drive home.

This was the first night of how I would live for the next three weeks; going to bars and getting completely obliterated every night. Taking the semester off from college before I started law school was the best decision I ever made. I thought I was having a great time and I even laughed when I saw a missed phone call from Charlie.

I strolled into my house around 3am after getting a ticket for losing my temper outside the bar with a random man. It was happening on and off, I was having fits of rage that I couldn't seem to control. The light in the living room was on. I turned the door knob to our front door; it was always unlocked. I walked into the spacious colonial-style home with Spanish tiles in the foyer, and the bamboo floors throughout the living and dining room. I stumbled through the foyer and into the dining room where my father was sitting at our grand 12 seat oak table.

"Hey, Dad. Why are you up so late?"

He looked up from his reading glasses. He's a tall man, like me, but has more of a blonde tint to his hair then red. I got the red hair from my mom. He has piercing blue eyes that would melt you on the spot if you didn't do what he asked.

"Your mother and I were talking tonight and we decided that you need to start getting your act together. Your 21 years old and all you've been doing since you turned 21 is drink and come home wasted. You went through your first four years of college free-of-charge and you didn't have a job the whole time.

"Dad, I worked at the hardware store in town since I was 16 and work part-time with you. That's a job."

He started to laugh. I knew when my dad started laughing it meant my argument was fruitless.

"If you think that's a job you're nuts." He pushed his chair out and stood up. He was about two inches taller than I am. "That's a job for a high school student not for a man. I know your plan is to go to law school; don't get me wrong, your mom and I are proud of you, we really are. We decided that you're going to have to get yourself through law school. You'll always have a place to stay and food to eat, but I'm not going to pay for your college anymore. You need to learn responsibility."

With that he pushed in his chair, walked out of the dining room, and up the stairs, leaving me speechless. I stepped into the living room, sat on the brown sectional, pushed the recliner up, and was imagining my dreams flying out the window. How am I going to do this on my own? I could see my future crumbling right before my eyes. Maybe I should call Charlie and talk to her. She always knew what to do. I looked at my phone and scrolled down to her name. I was about to push on it and then stopped myself. That may put me in a bigger hole. I crossed my arms over my chest and fell asleep.

~

I was awoken the next morning to my phone ringing. I let my voicemail pick it up. I sat up on the couch and placed my hands over my face. I had a pounding headache. I strolled into the solid-white kitchen with floor to ceiling windows that overlooked the Hudson River. My mom was sitting at the island in the center of the kitchen reading one of her favorite love stories that she could never put down.

"Good morning babe. Do you want breakfast?"

"Nope. I'm good." I sat next to her. "Were you involved in Dad's decision not to pay for law school?"

She put her book down. "I had to be. He's right. Ever since you stopped seeing Charlie you've done nothing, but mope around, and get drunk. It's not good for you. You have to get your life together."

"How am I supposed to get my life together if you and dad are cutting me off? I need money to get my life together. How am I supposed to pay for law school? It's going to be impossible." I grabbed a banana from the bowl of fruit. "I have to go to work. I'll see you later." I started to walk up stairs to get changed.

"Oh before I forget, Charlie's mom called this morning looking for you. She said she would try your cell phone."

I looked at my phone and noticed a missed call and a voicemail. Why would she be calling me? What if something happened to Charlie? I listened to the voicemail while I turned on the shower and took my clothes out for the day.

"Hello Jay. This is Mary, Charlotte's mother. Can you please give me a call when you get the message? I have a proposition for you."

I wonder what kind of "proposition" that psycho had for me. I always knew she was a little crazy when Charlie and I started dating. She was never concerned about how I was, as a person. All she was concerned about was the size of my wallet. She was very selfish, and I knew she wanted all three of her daughters to marry rich men. She wanted to make sure that she didn't have to support them for the rest of their lives.

I finished getting dressed and walked downstairs. My mom and dad where talking in the living room. I waved to them and walked out the door to my baby, my black 2013 Mustang. I opened the door and deeply inhaled the "Morning Fresh" air freshener I had hanging from the rearview mirror. I decided to call Mary on my way to work. Whatever she wanted shouldn't take that long; she usually gets right to the point.

Her cell phone rang twice before she answered, "Hello, Jay."

"Yes, Ms. Romeo. What can I do for you?"

I was waiting for her to tell me how much Charlie was missing me and that I needed to get back with her so she wouldn't go into a deep depression.

"For the hundredth time, call me Mary. Can we meet somewhere and talk? I can't talk about this over the phone."

"I'm on my way to work. Can we meet later on?"

"No. I'll call Bill and tell him you'll be late. It shouldn't be a problem. Meet me at the new bakery that just opened next to the library."

Before I couldn't say anything she hung up on me. I stared at the phone. Was she on some kind of drug? She was always so hyper.

Instead of going all the way down Main Street to the hardware store, I stopped at the small bakery that opened next to the library. It was a nice place with the iron chairs lined up outside for outdoor seating, and inside there was a long counter with all kinds of cookies, pastries, and a small area to sit, and eat. The place was quiet, except for Layla who was taking an order on the phone. She put her finger up to let me know she'd be right with me.

Layla grew up in Dobbs ferry. She's a few years older then me. She was very Italian-looking, with dark hair, dark eyes, and an olive complexion. She just reopened the bakery not too long ago and she remembered I loved the eclairs. Without even getting off the phone she went into the glass cabinet and pulled out an eclair for me. She placed it on a glass plate with a gold rim. I took the plate and gave her a thankful smile. I spun on my heels to turn around and found myself face-to-face with Mary. She's a short woman, topping off at around 5'1. She always wore platforms. Her skin was flawless and her make-up was perfect. She had shoulder length brown hair that she often wore in a ponytail, but today her hair was down and it reminded me so much of Charlie that I felt my stomach flip a little. I looked at my eclair and pushed it away.

"Would you like anything?"

"I don't eat this stuff. Just sit down in the back so we can speak privately." She glared at Layla who went into the back before Mary could make eye contact with her.

Mary's looks reminded me of Charlie, but this woman was cold. I was convinced that her heart was composed of a solid block of ice.

"What can I help you with, Mary?" When I was dating Charlie I would fix things around the house for her. I learned so much from working at the hardware store that I could probably open my own store if I couldn't afford law school.

"I need you to get back together with Charlie and I mean right away," she said nonchalantly.

Again, is this lady crazy? I just stared at her and realized she really was crazy.

"Mary, I don't mean to be rude or disrespectful, but I broke up with her because she was a high school fling. I care about her a lot. To start a relationship with her again, is just not worth the aggravation, and time."

"Jay, I don't think you understand. I didn't *ask* you to get back together with her I'm *telling* you to. I want you to come over to our house tomorrow. Tell her how much you love her, miss her, and that you want to be with her again."

"And why would I do that?"

"She's pregnant and the man that did this to her is a shady no good loser. I tried to get information about him, but the only thing that came up on the internet is a picture of his dead mother. She was murdered and the article said it was the boys fault.

"I'm sorry, Did you say she was pregnant?"

"Yes. I'm happy you're following along."

"I can't start dating her again, *especially* if she's pregnant with someone else's baby. You're going to have to find another person to agree with you and whatever you said on the phone about a proposition. I'm not up to doing this. I have to work and save up for school. My parents cut me off and I have to pay for Yale Law School.

I watched as the wheels in Mary's head started to turn. She placed her hand on her chin and smiled a very evil smile.

"Okay. How does this sound? You'll help me with my plan and in turn I'll pay for law school. We can go up to Connecticut and register for you to start immediately. It will be a cinch since I know the director of admissions."

I leaned back in my chair. It took me only a second to take in all the information before the same kind of cunning evil smile as Mary's splashed across my face. I slammed my chair back to the floor. "Okay Mary, you have a deal," I said.

"I'll meet you here tomorrow at 7:30am and we'll take a ride to Yale. I'll call the director and make an appointment for us. I'll give you all the details on the ride up."

I stood up, placed a five dollar bill on the counter for Layla, and walked out in the opposite direction from Mary. I got into my Mustang and felt the same ice that circled Mary's heart starting to form a thin layer around mine. This is perfect. It's just what I needed. What could possibly go wrong?

~

The morning came quickly. I didn't go out the night before. I knew I needed to be alert and on my game for the morning. I ran down the steps at 7:15am and my dad was in the kitchen.

"It's nice to see you were home and sleeping by 11pm for a change. I can tell our talk was good for you."

"Yes, it was. Thanks for the great talk and cutting me off. It will definitely make me a better person. You'll see."

I parked my Mustang by the Hudson River and walked up the steep hill. Mary was already waiting for me in her Mercedes truck.

"Good, I'm happy you dressed appropriately."

I had on a pair of dark gray slacks and a blue button shirt with my black pea coat. We were on the highway on our way to Yale before I could even start talking. Mary was a fast aggressive driver which suited her personality.

"So. Can you tell me a little about what's going on?"

"This is what I know: His name is Tommy Rhodes. He's a bartender in The Sports Bar in the city. Charlie met him in Club Aurora, and she went back to his house. He got her pregnant that night. I think he knew her family has money so he was setting himself up. He went to her first doctor's appointment with her and hasn't heard from him since. We need to keep it that way."

"So, what do you want me to do?"

"Just act like her boyfriend again. Keep her mind off this man. You can leave her when the baby is born. She'll be preoccupied; she's not going to care once the baby is born anyway. Then you're in law school, and I'll be a happy mother again. If you guys chose to stay together that's fine with me too. You know I always liked you."

"So that's it?"

"I also want you to find out more about Tommy Rhodes. I have a strange feeling he'll be back."

We pulled up to Yale. The director was waiting outside for us. He came up and opened Mary's door. He gave her a kiss on the cheek and shook my hand. He was average height and solidly built. He had a head full of black hair and gray eyes. He had a very firm, strong grip which I matched in our handshake. His smile was genuine unlike Mary's.

"So, Mary told me you wanted to sign up for law school. I actually found your application and it's spectacular. With your grades and SAT scores you'll not have a problem fitting into our program. Mary tells me your father owns the law firm Bushnell and Sons and you work there part-time. Are you thinking of following the footsteps of your father and brother?"

"I was hoping to be better, sir."

"Don't call me 'sir.' It makes me sound ancient. Call me Nick. Any friend of Mary's is a friend of mine. Please follow me. I'll register you myself. The fall semester has already started, but you can start our winter semester. It's a little more intense since the winter semester is rather short."

We followed him into the main entrance and took the elevator up to the third floor. He went over my classes with me. I decided to only take two in the winter. I wanted to excel and didn't want to overwhelm myself. As soon as registration was complete, Mary paid by credit card and our deal was sealed. I was enrolled in law school. I knew it would be a little of a commute, but it was going to be well worth it. I was on my way to becoming a lawyer.

~

The next morning was going to be the first time I would be seeing Charlie since I broke up with her. I wondered if she even looked pregnant yet. I told Mary that I would act surprised when she told me she was pregnant. I practiced what I was going to say in my mirror all morning. I knew Mary was making my dreams come true by paying for me to go to Yale. I decided not to tell my parents that I was enrolled for the winter. They would probably think I was selling drugs or something. Since, one minute I didn't have the money, and the next minute I'm registered, and have one semester completely paid for. I put on a pair of jeans and a white button-down shirt. I waved to my mom as I left and went straight to Charlie's house. I knew if I didn't do this quick I would chicken out. It was definitely something my better judgement was telling me I shouldn't do, but how do I not accept the proposition? Between Mary's insistent attitude and my parents severing my financial ties, I had been concerned. I had to accept. At least that's what I was telling myself.

I pulled up to Charlie's brick colonial house. Her parents were just as financially fortunate as mine. We used to compare our parent's salaries all the time. Charlie's father, Mel, was a cardiologist and Mary was the director of the Dobbs Ferry hospital. They were well-off. I looked at myself in the visor mirror and took a deep breath. "You can do this. You can do this," I said. I made sure I sprayed a healthy amount of her favorite cologne on myself before I left. The ocean scent lingering in my car. She loved the smell of the ocean. I walked up the path and rang the doorbell. Mary swung opened the door and yanked me into the foyer.

"Charlie, there's someone at the door who would like to speak to you," shouted Mary.

"Mom, I'll be right up." I heard Charlie say.

Hearing Charlie's voice made me feel warm inside. It brought back memories of how sweet she was to me. I took a deep breath as Mary looked at me and pushed me down into a seat.

"Jay, get it together. You're sweating."

I wiped my hand across my clammy forehead and took another deep breath to calm my nerves. It reminded me of when I picked Charlie up on prom night. She came walking down the steps in her navy blue dress. Her brown hair was done perfectly; not a strand out of place. She had just the right amount of make-up on. Her brown eyes glowed that night. I can remember it like it was yesterday.

I listened as I heard Charlie running up the steps from her basement apartment. She was probably writing in her journal. She was always scribbling in that thing. As she turned the corner a look of horror came over her face when she spotted me. Not a reaction I was expecting. Part of me thought she'd be happy to see me. I didn't know how to act so I stood up, straightened my posture, and smiled.

"What are you doing here?" she demanded.

"I just said I needed some space. I didn't say I never wanted to see you again," I tried to smile one of the smiles she liked.

"Oh! Well, this is not a good time."

"It's always a good time to see the love of your life! I think we need to talk."

She turned toward the basement. She might make a run for it. It doesn't seem like she wanted to see me at all. What was I doing? I turned to Mary who had the same evil smile on her face as the day in the bakery.

Charlie turned around to face me. "Okay come in. We can talk in my apartment."

I watched as she walked down the stairs. She didn't look pregnant at all. Could Mary have lied to me? I walked through the door that led to Charlie's apartment. My senses were immediately filled with the clean, flowery smell of this place....of Charlie. It made me feel nostalgic. I spent four years of my life in this apartment. Her mother had given it to her when she graduated high school. We were both so excited. We even talked about moving in together. I watched as Charlie walked into the kitchen, turned, and leaned on the counter. Man, she was beautiful.

"Charlie, Are you okay?"

"Sorry, Jay. I just have a lot on my mind since you left me in October."

"Well, anyway I was thinking that since Christmas was right around the corner, we could start our relationship back up. I mean I had my space to get my life together and you had your space to just relax and wait for me. What do you think?"

I watched as her face turned from peach, to pink, to dark red.

"Umm, Jay so much has changed since you left me. My life has become different."

"Different? It seems like everything is like it always was."

I looked around the apartment. The picture of the Hudson River during autumn was still hanging above her couch in the living room. We bought that picture together during a festival they had in Dobbs Ferry just last year. Charlie couldn't stop talking about how much she loved autumn. I had to buy it for her. I looked back at Charlie who was looking at the picture with me.

"The only thing different is that you seemed to have gained a little weight in your middle section, but that was probably from how upset you've been without me."

She shook her head and looked up at me with wide eyes. I hadn't convinced her yet. I pushed my hands through my hair.

"Our space? No Jay. You needed space. I never wanted space. Just one day out of nowhere you felt I wasn't worthy of you anymore. You didn't even give me an explanation about why you needed space."

"Charlie, I needed to get my life together. I can't work in my father's company forever. I decided to go to law school so we can have a good life together someday. It was done with good intentions."

I knew I had struck a chord with her. I watched her bite the inside of her mouth. She was thinking of what we once were, I knew it. It was taking her a while to answer me back. I took this opportunity to place a gentle kiss on her lips. Suddenly I wanted her; I couldn't help myself. I started pulling up her shirt and rubbing the deep arch of her back. I knew what she liked. I nuzzled my face by her shoulder so I could smell her hair that flowed gently down her back. It always smelled so sweet, like strawberries and cream. I rubbed her back harder and started pushing her body into mine. All the memories that came rushing back were uncontrollable. I really missed her.

"Jay please stop. We can't do this," she said breathlessly.

"Why not Charlie? Your mom's upstairs, she'll never hear a thing."

"It's not that. I'm pregnant."

She pushed me away. I had to think fast. I had to pretend I didn't know. I was afraid this was going to be the hardest part of this whole thing. I blurted out the first thing that came to my mind.

"Already we didn't even get that far yet." I joked, hoping she'd buy it. I started kissing her neck. "You're what!" I shouted for good measure.

"Jay, I'm so sorry. It wasn't my intention to hurt you or maybe it was but I never thought I would get pregnant. I just had one too many drinks that night. I'm so sorry."

"Charlie, stop rambling."

"I'm sorry I'm rambling. I just can't help myself," she said as she covered her mouth.

"Who was it Charlie?" I shouted. "We can't even take a break without you sleeping with someone else? Seriously, Charlie! I'm in shock. How many other guys did you sleep with? Five, 10 or maybe it was 20. You probably have no idea who the father is. I didn't think when I took your virginity that you would have the guts to sleep with the first guy that showed you some attention." I pushed my hands through my hair again.

"Get out! Get out now!" she shouted.

Maybe I took that too far.

"Charlie, wait don't get angry. You're in a very delicate situation right now. I'm so sorry. I didn't mean to hurt your feelings. I was just shocked by what you said."

"Please! You're the one that wanted space. You needed to get your life together. I thought I had my life together. I'm finished with my Bachelor's degree. I have my Masters program set up to study education. Finding out that I was pregnant totally ripped my life apart. In one night it seems my life did a complete turn-around. You just don't understand. Why don't you leave and take a lifetime of space?"

"Charlie, please don't kick me out. I love you! We can work this out together. The last thing I want or wanted to do is hurt you. I can't live without you. Please, we can work this out." As I said the words, I knew that they were true.

I pulled her in my arms and hugged her tight. I took her chin in my hands and slowly brought her lips to mine. I started kissing a trail down her neck and gently lifted her shirt and rubbed the arch of her back again. Charlie started kissing me harder. All the memories of the last three years poured through my mind. I wanted to be here. I belong here. I really do love her and I never want to leave her again. She stepped back and stared at me with those big, brown eyes as she untucked my shirt from my jeans. I couldn't take it anymore. I needed her. Impatiently I grabbed her by the back of the neck and thrust my lips onto hers with such force that she had no choice, but to kiss me back just as hard. I watched her step back as she took off her shirt and I unbuttoned my pants. I couldn't keep my hands off her. I scooped her in my arms and brought her into the bedroom. I saw the blue and white stripe comforter that my mom had given her when she first moved in strewn neatly across the bed. I gently placed her on the mattress. I have to remember that she is pregnant; we can't be as rough as we used to be. I stepped out of my pants and pulled hers down her smooth, slim legs. All thoughts of her being pregnant left my head when I pushed into her with such force that she cried out. When we were done she immediately started crying. I took her in my arms and rocked her back and forth like a small child who just fell and scraped her knee. I pushed her hair away from her face and kissed the salty tears off her cheeks.

"Charlie, I love you with all my heart. We will take care of this baby together. I just wanted to make that very clear to you."

"I know. I know you never stopped loving me. I'm just an emotional wreck right now," she cried.

I kissed her very gently until she fell asleep in my arms. This is what I needed. It was what we both needed. It was the biggest mistake of my life to leave her. I need her. Psycho Mary bringing us back together was fate. It had to be.

~

I peeked open my eyes as the sun was shining in through the window. I felt around to see if Charlie was next to me but she wasn't. Tomorrow, I started my first class at Yale, but today I will track Tommy Rhodes down and see what he's about. I took a quick shower and opened Charlie's closet. If I know her as well as I think, my clothes will still be in the back of the closet. I pushed all her clothes to one side and saw mine exactly where I'd left them. I put on a pair of gray colored jeans and a blue collared shirt. I grabbed my pea coat from the couch in the living room and walked upstairs.

"Oh! Hey, Jay...I didn't expect you." Annabel said.

Annabel is Charlie's younger sister. She has long brown hair, huge brown eyes, and she is also very attractive. Her body is slamming. There had been a few times when I was wondering what having a relationship with her would be like. If I put the moves on her right now she probably wouldn't stop me. She isn't the nice kind of girl that Charlie is; she's promiscuous.

"I was just hanging out with your sister."

"Oh good. Are you guys getting back together."

Before I could answer Mary was behind me, "Yes they are. Isn't it great?" She clasped her hands together. "Annabel, don't you have school or work or something?"

"I guess."

As Annabel was making her way up the stairs, Mary gave me a curl of her finger indicating that she wanted me to follow her. I walked into the living room.

"Okay. Tommy works at The Sports Bar. Go there and see what you can find out. He also rents a brownstone somewhere in the city. Find out more about that as well. I have a feeling this kid isn't going to keep away. Allow enough time to pass and he'll be back, I'm sure of it. It's your job to keep Charlie in love with you."

I nodded my head. It wasn't going to be hard to keep Charlie in love with me because I was in love with her again. Our relationship felt like it had never ended.

"She also has an appointment with her doctor soon. I'm sure she'll tell you about it. But make sure you go there with her."

I stuck my hands in my pockets and lifted my shoulders. I took my keys off the foyer table and went outside. It was a crisp day. Mild winds danced through the trees shaking the branches back and forth. Charlie was probably at work taking care of the two and three year olds that she loved so much. She's going to be a great mother. I hopped into my Mustang and started the car. I waited a few minutes for it to warm up and headed down to the city. It was going to be a long day.

My phone rang and I hit the speaker button.

"Hello."

"Hey Jay, it's Charlie."

I couldn't help the grin that formed across my face. "Hey sweetie. How's everything going?"

"Fine. I had a little break at work and just wanted to say that I really enjoyed last night."

"Charlie. I missed you. I'm happy I finally came to my senses and came back." I could hear her breath start to get heavier.

"Will I see you later?"

"Of course. I'm all yours."

"Jay, I love you."

"I love you too."

I hit the speaker button and drove down to the city with a permanent smile on my face.

There was very little traffic going into the city. Since I was down here I wanted to buy Charlie a Christmas present. She loved Christmas. I'll buy her a pair of diamond earrings. I pulled up to The Sports Bar. It was one of the only places in the city with a parking lot. I looked at my watch noting that it was lunch time. The perfect time to get something to eat, hang out by the bar, and watch football highlights. There were many cars parked in the parking lot, but only one car stuck out. It was a yellow Porsche Carrera, GT. I walked right up to it and gawked at it. This must be the owner's car. I walked up a few steps to the doors of the bar. I took a deep breath hoping that he had no clue who I was.

"Hello, welcome to The Sports Bar. How many?"

"Just one and I would like to sit at the bar."

"Sure the bar is right through the double doors."

I walked through the double doors and look around at the half full bar. I got lucky. A stool opened right in the corner that was right next to the back door. I kept my coat on. It was definitely a little chilly in here, but just in case I wanted to sneak out I could. I could see two of the TVs and was in great position to see everyone at the bar. There was a tall lady with blonde hair stocking up the bar. I didn't see any men in the bar area. She came toward me when I made eye contact with her.

"Hey, can I get you something to drink?"

"I'll have a Coors light draft and a menu, please."

She handed me a menu and came back a second later with my Coors light.

"I'll give you a second too look at the menu. If you need anything I'm Lori….and if you don't see me, Tommy should be in any minute."

"Thanks."

Luck was on my side today. I took my time looking at the menu. I wanted to wait until Tommy came in to order. I looked around and took in the atmosphere of the bar. There were signed baseballs in a display case behind the bar. I even noticed signed basketballs and framed jerseys scattered around the bar area.

"Hey can I get you something to eat?"

I looked up and I knew immediately that this was the famous Tommy standing in front of me. Right in front of me was the man that got my Charlie pregnant.

"I would like a Reuben sandwich with a side of onion rings and another Coors light draft."

I watched him as he placed my order in the computer. Mary was right. This kid was out for Charlie and her money. He was tall but not as tall as me. He had wavy blonde hair and piercing blue eyes. He had on a pair of khaki shorts and a dark blue polo shirt with the collar flipped up a little. He was definitely a punk. He handed me my beer and put out his hand.

"By the way, I'm Tommy. Are you new around here? I never saw you before."

"Just passing through."

"I didn't catch your name."

"My name is Jay."

"Great. If you need anything just get me."

I was curious to know who's Porsche was outside, "Hey, Tommy. Do you know who's yellow Porsche that is outside? It's a beauty."

He just laughed.

The Porsche was his. Maybe Mary was wrong about him. I drank my beer slowly as I watched people come and go. I ate my Reuben and was getting ready to leave when two men walked in and sat two stools away from me. They had a long cylindrical container. Tommy walked up to them and shook both their hands. The shorter of the men opened the cylinder and pulled out blue prints. I was close enough to hear their conversation.

"These are the drawings that you requested Mr. Rhodes."

I watched as Tommy took them and laid them flat onto the bar. From what I could see they looked like plans for another restaurant or bar.

"These are perfect. Can I take them so Lori can go over them as well?"

"Yes, Mr. Rhodes. These are for you to keep."

He shook the man's hand and placed the cylinder across the bar. I had to get those blue prints. Luck was on my side because just then Tommy went into the back room. This was my opportunity to act fast and quick. I grabbed the long cylinder and exited out the back door. I didn't even pay my bill. I jumped into my Mustang and peeled out. My heart was racing. I never did anything like that before. It felt kind of good.

I blasted the radio on the ride home. When I pulled up to my house I ran up to my room, opened up the cylinder, and laid the blueprints on the table. It was plans for another restaurant. It said opened by 2014 and design by Jones and Son, Greenport, New York. Greenport was out on Long Island. I wonder why he was dealing with people from Greenport.

~

It was January already. It hasn't snowed yet, but you could feel it coming soon. Today I'm going to Charlie's doctor's appointment. She's excited. I'm not sure what I am yet. I drove to her house. I went to honk the horn, but she was already outside. She leaned over and gave me a kiss on the cheek. We arrived 15 minutes early for the appointment. I followed Charlie to the receptionist's desk.

"Hello, Lynn. I would like to check in," Charlie said.

"Of course. We aren't very busy today so Dr. Castano can see you on time," Lynn said with a smile.

I cleared my throat. Pretty rude of her not to introduce me.

"Oh, Lynn this is my boyfriend, Jay. Jay this is Lynn."

"A pleasure to meet you," Lynn said.

"Same here," I said.

I took Charlie's hand and we walked to the waiting area together.

Do you like it so far?" Charlie asked.

"I guess." I wasn't quite sure what she wanted me to like.

"Are you excited?" she said.

I ignored her. Charlie would sometimes ramble when she was nervous and the 50 questions were probably part of her nervousness. I looked at Charlie. She was so cute. She didn't even look pregnant. All last month it didn't even feel like she was pregnant.

"You know Charlie I was thinking of going out somewhere. Since you're not showing too much maybe we could go to a club and go dancing. Maybe Club Bombay? What do you think?"

"Jay, I don't know."

Before I could ask her why, a lady came into the waiting room and started barking orders at Charlie. She was talking so fast that I didn't even understand what she was saying. I tried to follow Charlie into the bathroom, but she waved for me to follow the nurse. I walked into a room that had a table with legs coming out from the side. I cringed when I figured what was going to happen on that table. I sat in the chair across from it, took out my phone, and started doing research on Greenport, New York. I found out that Tommy and his sister Lori own The Sports Bar in the city and the blue prints were of the next bar they were opening together. I also called Jones and Son and pretended to be a building inspector from the city. There are many in the city, so what would a small architecture firm in Greenport know? I asked if Mr. Rhodes owned any more property and they had no problem telling me they owned a bed and breakfast in Greenport. I already had a phone call out to them.

Charlie came in and looked like she had seen a ghost. I look around wondering if I did something wrong. I could see her eyes starting to get watery. It made me wonder if she was thinking of Tommy. He did come to her first doctors appointment. Charlie was never good at hiding her feelings. She smiled a very weak smile at me.

"If I were you I would sit by my head. You really don't want to watch from that angle," she said.

I smirked at her and glanced at the table. I half-listened as Nurse Kim came in and talked to Charlie. She only gained two pounds and she gets headaches. I picked up the parenting magazine and started flipping through it. There was a slight knock on the door and a plain looking lady with her brown hair in a ponytail walked in.

"Good morning," the doctor said. "Okay we have blood work to do today. I'm going to test you for gonorrhea and chlamydia. I will also start testing your urine for proteins. Do you have any questions before we get started?"

What? Why would they have to test her for any of that? I watched as Charlie climbed on the table and put her feet in the legs that came out of the side of the table. I slipped my hand in my pocket and hit the ringer.

"Oh, I'm sorry I have to get this. It's an important call. Please don't wait for me."

Charlie gave me the look of death as I walked out saying, 'hello' into my phone. I walked to my car and sat in it. I watched as she walked out of the doctor's office 15 minutes later. I could tell she was annoyed.

"Why didn't you come back in?"

"I don't know, Charlie. I was kind of grossed out when she started talking about sexually transmitted diseases and then wanted to test you for them."

"Jay, that's routine. They even test you when you're married. Please Jay, I don't want to talk about this."

"Well, maybe I do. Charlie, what happens if you have something. You know like something..."

She cut me right off. I hated when she did that.

"It didn't seem like you cared about that a few weeks ago when you were dying to get back into my pants. Just take me home."

I can't believe she said that. I felt we were doing fine. I didn't pressure her to have sex because I knew she was pregnant. I didn't want her to feel uncomfortable.

~

The winter was here and it was brutal out. Charlie was three months pregnant and she was starting to show. Law school was going great, Charlie and I decided to move in together and I was in love with her again. It was like I never left. I put my arms around her slightly swollen abdomen.

"Charlie, let's go out somewhere before you start to really show."

"I would love to go dancing," she said.

"Get a few of your girlfriends together and we can all go to a club in the city."

"That sounds great!" she said.

She was excited. She ran into the room and shut the door. I went upstairs to Mary's part of the house and decided to shower there. Since I moved in I kept my clothes in an empty bedroom. It was easier since Charlie's apartment was fine for her, but too crowded for us. I had my towel wrapped around my waist ready to get into the shower when Mary walked out of her bedroom.

"We haven't touched base in a while. Did you find out anything?"

"Mary, I think this is getting ridiculous. It's been two months and this man never came around. I don't think he's interested in Charlie. It was a one night fling and that was it."

"It seems like someone is falling in love again."

"You're right. I am. I love her."

"Will you be willing to love the baby as well?"

"Why would I not love a baby that's mine?"

Mary started laughing as she threw her head back. "I want the rest of the information on Tommy. It may be for my own pleasure to know what he's about."

"I don't think I want to do it anymore."

"And I don't think I want to pay for law school anymore. By what Nick, the director of the program said, you're doing wonderfully in the law program. I wouldn't mess it up if I were you."

She walked back into her room and slammed the door. I jumped into the shower and was dressed in 15 minutes with blue jeans, a white button down shirt, and a blue blazer. I walked down stairs as Charlie walked out of her bedroom.

I couldn't help but to stare at her because she looked just beautiful.

"Charlie, you look stunning in your little black dress."

"Don't lie to me. Just tell me the truth. I look like a fat elephant."

I pushed her hair behind her ear. I could feel her heartbeat quickening. As I whispered, "Okay Porky, you look like an elephant...especially with those flats on, so can you please put on heels? This will most likely be the last time you'll be able to wear a pair of heels."

"You're right! Like always."

She walked out in the black pumps that I bought her for Christmas since I never got her the earrings.

I didn't even have to ask her who we were picking up. Her only friend was Marisa. She was always content with just the one friend and I never minded Marisa. She was a little of a gossip queen, but she was never out to hurt anyone. We pulled up to Marisa's house and her and Annabel were sitting outside. Immediately they started talking about the baby and how Charlie felt. I started laughing when the girls kept on saying how great Charlie looked. I really thought she was finally starting to show.

"And what are you laughing at?" Charlie asked.

"I'm not laughing at you. I was thinking you're already showing. It must be all those tacos you're eating."

"Ha! Ha! You're so hilarious. How about your belly? It seems to be growing with mine."

We laughed all the way to Club Bombay. Club Bombay was my favorite club. It reminded me of us. Charlie and I used to come here all the time. My cousin was a bouncer and snuck us in all the time. He told us we weren't allowed to talk or socialize with anyone and of course, no drinking. The first few weekends we didn't, but then we started to drink and have a great time. We got so wasted the last time we were there that I had to leave my Mustang parked on the street because Charlie insisted we take a cab home. She didn't want me drinking and driving. When we went back the next morning, my car was gone. It had been towed. I was furious that I had to spend money to get the car back.

I looked over and I could see Charlie was crying. I could see she was trying to hide it from me so I pretended I didn't notice. We pulled up to Club Bombay. I called Charlie's name twice.

"Charlie, snap out of it!" I said. "You're in one of those really deep stares again."

"We're here," Annabel said.

"I'm going to valet park the car so you don't have to walk a long way," I said.

"Thank you," Charlie said as she kissed me on the cheek.

I went to park the car in the lot across the street and walked right into the club. I slipped the bouncer 20 dollars. I didn't want to wait on the long line. The bar was packed. I saw a few people I knew and then spotted Charlie waving at me. I never liked to dance. I always had a friend when I went out to bars because Marisa hated to dance also. I watched Charlie as she danced with Annabel.

"How are things going?" Marisa asked as she looked at me with her catlike green eyes.

She was always very attractive but her gossiping got her into trouble with the boys in school. None of them ever wanted to date her. I would never tell Charlie this and I know Marisa would never either but I did sleep with Marisa when Charlie and I first started dating. It was a quick, drunken thing, and we were both very sorry that we did it.

We both swore never to tell Charlie about it. I guess that's why I'm not horribly upset that she slept with someone else. We're even now. Except for the pregnancy thing, but it didn't matter now.

"Things are going great, Marisa. How's everything with you?"

We always had an awkward relationship and we both knew it was because of our secret. I was half listening to Marisa talking to me about how I felt about becoming a father when I saw him.

I watched as Charlie's face lit up.

I watched him talk to her and her talk back to him.

Even Annabel was laughing and talking to him.

I slowly started to make my way to them as he reached for her arm. Charlie took a few steps back as her face turned completely white. I made my way faster through the crowd. I was pushing men and women out of my way.

"Hey. Watch out! Stop pushing."

I didn't even look back. I saw red. I needed to get to Charlie. I grabbed her hand she turned around and I could see the tears starting to form in her eyes.

"Charlie, I saw that guy grab you. I wanted to make sure you were okay."

"Jay, I'm fine. It was just some drunken guy trying to dance with us. Annabel handled it. I'm just feeling a little lightheaded. It must be the lights. I would just like to go home."

I scanned the dance floor and made eye contact with Tommy as I pushed Charlie through the crowd. She was out of it, I practically dragged her to the car. I dropped Marisa off at her house. Annabel helped me with Charlie. She opened the front door as I scooped Charlie into my arms and carried her down the stairs and tucked her into bed. Mary was right. This guy was going to come back into her life. I needed to find out more and soon. Judging from the way Charlie looked at him, I knew she liked him more then she let on.

~

A week had gone by and Charlie seemed back to her old self. I woke up that morning to find Charlie in the kitchen making coffee. I walked over and put my arms around her.

"Jay, I need some time away. I really would like a vacation, but my sister's house will have to do."

"Charlie, what do you need to think about? I think everything is going well," I waited for her to answer me. I wondered if she's been in touch with Tommy and is hiding something from me.

"Jay, please don't look at me that way. It's not you. Marisa, Annabel, and I are going up to Chappaqua to my sister's house for a weekend, just to hang. You know, just the girls."

"It was that guy at the club last weekend wasn't it? Ever since you saw him you have been in another world. Who was he, Charlie?"

"Jay, what guy?"

I can't believe she was lying right to my face. I could feel my heart pumping hard in my chest. I imagined myself hurting her. I could just push her it wouldn't be a big deal. I snapped myself out of it.

"Oh Charlie, you know exactly who I'm talking about. I can tell you're nervous, you're biting the inside of your cheek."

"Please, Jay, just stop it. You're imagining things." She patted my face like I was a puppy dog. I could feel my insides boiling. "And stop giving me those eyes. I'll see you Sunday night," She now spoke to me like I was a child and kissed me like I was her friend.

"Charlie, you just seem a little distant this week."

"Jay, I love you. Stop thinking and go have fun somewhere with your friends."

Oh yeah. I'm going someplace real fun this weekend. I waved to her as she got into Marisa's car. I grabbed my overnight carrier and packed clothes for one night. I decided to take a rode trip to Greenport, New York. I wanted to see the bed and breakfast that Tommy owned. I received a phone call from a girl named Kate just a few days ago. I reserved a room for the night. When I knew Charlie was well on her way to her sister's house I jumped into my Mustang and started on my way to the bed and breakfast. It took me less than two hours to get there. When I pulled up I could see the sign for the bed and breakfast swinging as the wind blew. When I walked up the path I could see in small letters above the door that read *The Bartlett House*. It was an old-fashioned Victorian house. I knocked once before I noticed that the door was cracked opened. I walked in to a warm, inviting reception area.   Standing at the counter was a gorgeous lady with dark hair and blue eyes.

"Hello, can I help you?"

"Yes, I have a reservation in your single suite."

"Oh yes. You must be Jason Bushnell."

"Yes, ma'am."

"Please call me Abby."

Abby looked up. She had a dazzling smile.

"Let me give you the itinerary for the weekend."

"Oh that's okay. I'm only going to be here for the night."

"That's fine. We are serving lunch at 12:00 in the parlor and dinner at 6:00 in the sunroom. You're our only guest tonight." She smiled. "Follow me I'll take you to your room."

I followed her up a flights of stairs and into the second room on the left. She opened the door with a key and then handed it to me.

"Enjoy."

"Thanks."

The room was small. There were veranda doors leading to a small balcony that displayed a view of the Long Island Sound. It was chilly, but beautiful regardless. There was a double bed in the corner, a night stand, and a dresser with six draws. I walked into the bathroom and turned on the shower. I stood under the hot water for 20 minutes. I closed my eyes and tried to relax. My mind was racing. I couldn't get Charlie out of my head. I was having images of her in bed with Tommy. I shook my head and squeezed my eyes shut. I turned off the water as I was trying to catch my breath. I grabbed the towel off the hook and wrapped it around my waist. I placed my hands on the sink and took slow breaths. The steam was helping, but not enough. I walked out of the bathroom and opened the veranda doors. The air was chilly. I had goosebumps all over, but I was sweating. I closed my eyes tight again when I got the same image of Charlie and Tommy. I quickly went back inside the warm room, got dressed, and walked to the parlor for lunch.

"Good afternoon," a chubby, round faced woman said.

"Hey," was all I managed to say.

I wiped my forehead as sweat started to drip down. I could feel my heart racing.

"Are you okay sir?"

I could hear the chubby lady speaking as the room started to spin.

"Just. Need. A drink. P-P-lease."

I felt her push me into the chair. She came back instantly and stuck a straw in my mouth. I took a deep long sip. I could feel my head beginning to clear up. What's just happened to me?

"Hey, can you hear me?"

"Yeah. I have a pounding headache."

"I'll get you some pain medicine. It looked like a really bad anxiety attack."

I hope that's what it was.

"Let me bring you some of my chicken noodle soup."

I shook my head. I grabbed hold of my head. Maybe I'm just stressed out between law school, Charlie, becoming a new father, Mary, and now Tommy. I could feel myself coming back to reality. The room stopped spinning, the rainbow of colors was gone, and my vision became clearer. The chubby lady came back with my soup. She placed it in front of me along with the headache relief pills.

"I'm sorry, but I didn't catch your name?" I said.

"It's Kate. You have some really bad anxiety. The chicken soup should make you feel better. I get anxiety too. It was really bad when my mom died, but I can control it better now."

"Can you please sit with me until I feel better?"

She smiled at me. "Sure."

"Thanks."

I was scared. When it came to strange things that happened to me I would always get scared. When I was younger I used to get cluster headaches. Every time I would get them my mom would let me lay in her bed until I felt better. I remembered my heart beating very fast and not being able to catch my breath.

"So where are you from?" Kate asked.

I started to remember why I was here. "Oh, I'm from the city."

"You are. My brother lives there."

"Oh cool."

"The city is such a large place you probably wouldn't know him," she said giggling.

"It is a big place, but you never know."

"His name is Tommy Rhodes."

"Oh yeah. I know him. Him and his sister, Lori, own a bar on broadway."

"Yes, that's them. What a small world. You're in luck! He's on his way down tonight. He should be here by dinner."

I could feel my heart starting to race again. My hands were getting clammy. Why is this happening to me?

"Are you okay? It looks like you saw a ghost," I heard Kate say.

"I'm fine," I said in between gulps of water. I'm just going to go and lay down."

I walked up the stairs and into my room in a complete daze. What was I doing here? I didn't even come down here with a plan. Okay, I found out he owns a bed and breakfast, and has one gorgeous sister, and one heavy one. What did I accomplish here? I packed up my bag and decided I had to go. I walked down the stairs. Abby the pretty one was by the reception desk.   She looked me right in my eyes and then down at my bag.

"Leaving so soon?"

"Yes. I think I'm coming down with something."

"My sister told me you didn't look good during lunch."

"She's right. Like I said, I must be coming down with something."

"Well, you're more than welcome to stay here and just relax in your room until the morning. You don't have to rush out of here. We're empty tonight."

"I think I'll go. Thanks for your hospitality."

She shrugged her shoulders, and gave me the receipt for the half day stay at the Bartlett House.   I left that afternoon realizing I accomplished nothing and risked getting caught by Tommy.   I went through the town and parked the car.   It was a very touristy town.   I walked passed an old fashioned school house that I knew Charlie would love.   I walked across the street and stopped in.   Man, this place must be old. I walked up to the front and there was a bulletin board with the weeks activities in the town.   They were having a concert in Mitchell Park tonight. I assumed that's why Tommy is coming down, so he could hang out and listen to music in the park. What a loser.

I pushed open the door and saw it was set up like a meeting hall.   There were rows of folding chairs. I walked halfway into the room when I started getting that feeling again. I was envisioning Charlie and Tommy walking hand in hand in the park listening to the music. I was so disoriented. I tried to take deep breaths. Nothing was calming the feeling I had in the pit of my stomach. I placed my hands on the first chair I saw to try and relax myself, but instead I picked it up and flung it against the others. I kicked the other standing chairs down. I was yelling and crying at the top of my lungs. I felt a strong grip grab my wrist and then I was on the floor being restrained by a woman.

"What the heck do you think your doing?" the woman asked.

I took more deep breaths, closed my eyes tight, and then opened them back up. It took me a second for my vision to focus on the woman with the black eyes and side-braided black hair.

"I don't know. I got a really bad headache. Please don't call the police. I couldn't take the pain of the headache. It's like a sharp pain that comes very quickly. The pain brings me to my knees." I stood up and pulled my arm out of her hand. "I'm fine now."

"You came in here all calm and then started kicking the chairs that I just finished setting up and screaming like a psychopath. Now you're going to clean up my chairs and line them all back up the way they were or I'll call the cops. You should go see a doctor for those headaches. They sound like cluster headache to me. But I ain't no doctor."

"I will."

I started picking up the chairs when I noticed a picture on the wall. The picture looked familiar, but I couldn't place the lady in the picture.

"Excuse me," I yelled.

The lady came running back. "What?"

"Who's this lady?" I pointed to the pretty blonde's picture that was hanging on the wall.

"That's Mrs. Cindy Rhodes. She was a big leader in the community. She use to run The Bartlett House."

There was a plaque above her picture that read, *In memory of Cindy Rhodes.* "What happened to her?"

"She was murdered on the beach by some clan leader about seven years ago. It was rumored that her son got her killed."

"Her son?"

"Yes, her son's name is Tommy Rhodes."

"He got her killed? How?"

"He was part of this Wicca clan and he disobeyed the leader and supposedly the leader killed his mother. But it's all rumors. You never know what to believe anymore." The lady looked around the room. Don't forget to finish up."

I couldn't believe how much Tommy looked like his mom. It was a sad story but if he got his mom killed he could also get Charlie killed. I have to get home.

I picked up the last chair. "Hey ma'am I'm leaving now."

"Bye now. Take care of those headaches," she yelled from a room in the back.

I had no idea what was going on with my brain. They were definitely headaches, but I was also getting very disoriented. I knew I was kicking the chairs and throwing them. It felt like I was out of my body while I was doing it. It was weird. I got back in my car and headed home. I slept at my parents house for the night.

~

I pulled into the driveway just in time to see Marisa's Volvo pull out of the driveway. I opened the front door.

"Charlie, is that you?" I said.

"Yes, I'll be out in a minute."

Charlie came out a few minutes later. Her eyes were red rimmed and she was sniffling slightly. I knew it couldn't have been Tommy because he was on his way to Greenport.

"Are you crying?"

I went over to hug her, but she pushed me away.

"Charlie, what did I do? You go out with your girlfriends, get upset about something, and now you're blaming me?"

I pushed her out of the way, went into the bathroom and slammed the door. I came out an hour later. I peeked into her room to find her asleep. I snuck upstairs to see if Mary was still awake. She was always up late. Even when we were younger we would come in from a late night and there was Mary sitting at the kitchen island sipping tea, or eating a bowl of cereal.

I slowly opened the basement door. I didn't want Annabel to see me. Sure enough, Mary was sitting at the kitchen island sipping a glass of milk. She made eye contact with me and waved me into the kitchen.

"We have to talk quietly. Annabel just went to bed a little while ago."

I check the time it was only 9:30pm.

"I went to The Bartlett House and found out it's owned by Tommy Rhodes. His sisters run it. His mother was also murdered, but you already knew that. I showed you the blueprints of the new bar he is opening...and that's about it. I don't think there is really anything else. It doesn't seem like he's coming back. It's been a while since I saw him at the club. I think we're fine."

"Jay, just so you know I told Nina what was going on between the two of us."

Nina was Charlie's older sister. She was the calm one. She was the peacemaker. It became obvious that Mary was feeling guilty about something since she told Nina about our deal."

"You told her that your paying for my law school?"

"Yes, I also told her I have you on a mission to find out about this lunatic that got Charlie pregnant."

"And what did she say about it?"

"Nothing. She won't say anything. I made her promise she wouldn't."

Like that meant anything. It's sad that Mary knows nothing about her daughters and how close they are. When Mary tells one of them something they all tell each other and then keep everything from Mary. I know Nina told Charlie. I have to see and watch for signs.

"You think she'll keep the secret?"

"Of course. Nina never disobeys me." She smirked. "I'm going to bed."

I walked back down to the basement, put on my boxer briefs, crawled into bed next to Charlie, and fell asleep.

~

Charlie woke me up early so I could shovel the drive way. She didn't want to slip on her way to her doctor's appointment. I came in blowing on my ice cold hands.

"Charlie, hurry up we're going to be late for your doctor's appointment," I yelled as I pulled off my shirt and grabbed a dry one.

We drove to the doctors in silence. We pulled up to the building, Charlie hopped out and started walking into the office without me. Dr. Castano's office was packed. Two chairs in the corner were free.

"Charlie, what's on your mind lately?" I asked.

"Nothing! I'm just excited to find out what the sex of the baby is."

"That's it?" I looked her up and down.

"Why? Is there something you need to talk to me about?"

"Umm....no, it's just you've been acting weird since you came back from your sister's house. I was just wondering if something happened while you were there."

I watched as her face turned a deep red.

"No, Jay nothing happened. I just had a very relaxing weekend." The sarcasm in her voice was noticeable.

The nurse called us in and did the regular routine with Charlie. I vaguely heard the nurse say her blood pressure was high. I can't understand what she has to be stressed out about. She lives a very easy life. She only works part time now. She is mostly home. What does she really have to be stressed out about? I watched as Dr. Castano walked in and started talking to Charlie about the baby. I didn't really care for the doctor's appointments. They did the same thing every time.

My phone rang in my pocket. I saw Mary's name in bright blue letters.

"Charlie, I have to take this phone call. Can we wait to do this?"

I waited as she looked at the doctor and then they both looked at me.

"I would rather just get this over with. I'm really excited to find out what we're having. Go take your phone call. I'll tell you everything when I come out."

I gave her a kiss on the cheek, waved at Dr. Castano, and left the office.

I called back Mary immediately.

"Jay, I'm happy you called me back. Nina told Charlie everything."

"What?"

"You heard me. Trust me I'm very annoyed at Nina. This is the first time she ever went against me."

I quietly shut the phone. This lady just ruined my life. Charlie knew I was looking for Tommy. She knows I got back together with her because her mother was paying for my law school tuition. I stared into space and felt my head getting hot and heavy. I took a few deep breaths to gain control of myself. I imagined Nina talking to Charlie about everything that happened. They were probably in their pajamas eating popcorn talking about me the whole time. I pushed my hands through my hair. I saw Charlie starting to walk out and I placed the phone back by my ear. I was trying as hard as I could to calm myself down. I wanted to kill Mary and her idiotic ideas. I watched as Charlie walked to the car. She started to flip the door handle impatiently, but I had to calm down a little more. I didn't want to snap on her. I took one last breath and placed my phone back in my pocket.

"Sorry. The phone call was very important," I said.

"More important than my doctor's appointment?"

I could see how red her face was getting. Maybe her blood pressure is high. She walked up to me and pointed her finger at my chest.

"Charlie, get your finger away from me."

"Why don't you tell me the truth? Why are you really back with me?"

"Charlie, what are you talking about?"

I could kill Mary right now.

"Did you think I wasn't going to find out? Did you think my mother or sisters were going to be able to keep a secret? Haven't you been around my family enough to know that there is no such thing as privacy or secrets in my house? Before you agreed with one of my mother's bright ideas think about it first."

She was now screaming at the top of her lungs. I looked around as everyone was looking at us and she knew I hated it when she made a scene.

"Charlie, get in the car and we'll talk about it," I said through clenched teeth.

"No, Jay I'm finished talking about it. I don't think I care about what you have to say. Why don't you get your last pay check from Mary, and get out of my apartment?"

I got in my car and floored it. Let that bitch walk home. She didn't even want me to explain anything. This was all Mary's fault. I got to the apartment before her. I walked out as she was coming in. I left with a small bag.

I ignored her as she yelled, "I don't think that's all your stuff."

I slammed the door in her face.

I drove back to my parents house, walked into the front door, and slammed it hard. I couldn't control myself any longer. I couldn't believe this was happening to me.

~

I sat on my bed trying to come up with how to explain
this to Charlie. I didn't want her to leave me. I decided to go
to her house in the morning to explain what happened. It
was all her mother's fault. I was just a victim in this whole
fiasco. It was all Mary's fault.   Charlie and I should confront
her. What was the big deal now? Law school was going
great. If I convinced Charlie that it was Mary's fault then we
could persuade Mary to finish paying for my law school. I
walked to my closet and sat on the floor. I ran my fingers
through the floor boards like I did many times and pulled at
the loose one. I put my hand in the hole and pulled out a
bottle of vodka, pills that controlled my bipolar disorder, and
a picture of Charlie. Being Bipolar was one of my secrets
growing up. My parents suspected something when I was
five and because I would have awful temper tantrums that
were uncontrollable. I remember them taking me to Doctor
Park. He was a specialist in temper tantrums. He told my
parents I would grow out of it. There was nothing wrong with
their precious five-year-old. When I was twelve I would go
into my mother's room and tell her that my brain wouldn't
calm down. It was like my brain was in a race. I couldn't
make my thoughts leave my head or stop them from going
so fast. My mother took me to another specialist, Dr.
Freebody. She specialized in neurological problems in
adolescents. She told them to keep an eye on me and
monitor my outbursts. If it got worse they would do a whole
work-up. It ended when I was 14. I was hypomanic and I
was showing signs of grandiose behavior. It was like I had a
larger-then-life feeling. I felt superior. Nothing could stop
me.   I left my house in the middle of the night and took the

bus to Washington Heights. I got off the bus in the middle of a rundown neighborhood and started walking with my chest puffed out like I owned the neighborhood. I walked past gangs of people unafraid. I woke up the next morning in the hospital with two broken ribs, a broken nose, and many bruises. When the doctors asked me what happened I couldn't remember. It was like I completely blacked out. The last thing I could remember was going into my kitchen in the middle of the night getting a glass of water. The doctors decided I had bipolar disorder. I knew there was something wrong with my brain since I was five-years-old. I stayed on the medication from the time I was 14 until I turned 18. When I settled into my life, I begged Dr. Freebody to let me stop taking the medicine. I told her my life was perfect. I had a great girlfriend, I was in college, and everything was perfect. I was fine because Charlie loved me. Everything started going downhill for me again when Mary came into my life with this ridiculous proposition.

I popped a pill in my mouth and took a swig of vodka. I woke up the next morning feeling groggy. I stumbled down my steps and into my car. I drove to Charlie's house. I parked around the corner and walked into her house to find it empty. I checked the clock. It was 9am. Where was she? I got a drink of water when I heard a car. Tommy's yellow Porsche was pulling into the driveway. I started grinding my teeth really hard; my hands formed into fists and then I stopped in my tracks. I took a few deep breaths and talked myself out of running outside and completely losing my mind. I was calm and I was going to stay calm. I took my medicine last night to stop my manic behavior.

I waited by the door as she turned the knob and practically walked right into me. I wanted to take her by the shoulders and fling her to the ground and kick her until she was dead. I shook my head and got rid of those thoughts.

"Who was that driving that Porsche?" I said.

"Marisa's dad. What are you doing back here?"

You lying little slut!

"My first class was cancelled; I dropped my car off for an oil change down the block and figured I would get a few more things."

"A few more things? Why don't you just take everything?"

"I don't have my car with me. I'll be back to pick up the rest of my things."

I kissed her goodbye on the cheek and left. I was determined to talk to Charlie but I had to find the right time. I went back to my house.

My mom was sitting in the living room. "Hey, Jay. How's law school going?" She asked. I ignored her. I didn't want to talk or deal with anyone right now. I went back into my closet and took another few swigs of vodka. I dropped two pills into my hand and threw them into my mouth and took another gulp of vodka to wash them down. I sat there until I felt calm. I walked back down the steps and drove my Mustang to Dobbs Ferry Hospital. I had to talk to Mary. I went up to the eighth floor. Her secretary, Doreen was sitting at her desk, swamped with mountains of paper around her.

"Hello, Jay. How can I help you?"

"I need to see Mary," I said through clenched teeth.

Doreen came from around her desk. She looked frightened. Did I look that scary? She knocked on Mary's door and then peeked her head in. She went back to her desk.

"Jay you can go right in."

I didn't say anything to her. I knocked on the door and walked right in. Mary was sitting at her oval conference desk with papers around her.

"Please have a seat."

I pulled out the chair that was on wheels and went to sit down. The chair slid out from under me and I hit the floor. Mary jumped up to help me, but I was already on my feet.

"We need to talk," I said as I slowly sat on the seat.

"What's going on with you? You don't look great?"

"I'm not doing well. She was with him last night."

"With who?"

I slammed my fist on the table. "With Tommy Rhodes that's who. Is there another "him" I should know about?"

"No. I just didn't think he was going to come back around. It's been a while."

"Well, he came back and Charlie kicked me out."

Mary's eyes went wide. "Oh, she did."

"What are you going to do about it?" I asked.

"Why don't you confront them and have her choose who she wants to be with? She loves you. How long has she known this other guy for? She will definitely choose you. Go now and wait for her."

I listened to Mary like she was the Almighty One. It sounded like she knew what she was talking about. I left her office in a daze and went back to my car, and to Charlie's house. I parked my car around the corner. I expected to have trouble getting the door opened but the front door was slightly opened. The locks were changed. It seems like whoever changed them never closed the door all the way. I saw boxes by the garage. I opened one of them. It was filled to the rim with my clothes. I closed it back up and brought it back into the house. I waited at the kitchen table for her to come home. I kept checking my watch. She never came home that night. I opened up one of the boxes she packed with my clothes in it and placed some back in the closet. I crawled into her bed and fell fast asleep.

I woke up sweating and breathing heavy. I must have had a nightmare. I haven't woken up like this is a long time. I looked at the clock it was noon. I jumped up and ran into the kitchen. Charlie was still not home. I made a decision to find her. I took out my phone and called The Sports Bar. It rang twice before someone picked up.

"Thanks for calling The Sports Bar. How can I help you?"

"I need to speak to a manager."

"Hold on a second while I transfer you."

I waited on hold listening to a beeping sound. They couldn't even put music on for the people that were on hold."

"Hello, this is Thomas. How can I help you?"

I knew he wasn't one of the managers. He was the head waiter. That means Lori isn't there either.

"I would like to know when the bartender with the blonde hair will be in next."

"I'm not sure. The managers are away for the weekend in Greenport. Can I help you with anything?"

"No thanks. I just enjoyed his company last time I was there."

I hung up and squeezed my phone. Yes, Thomas you did help me.

I walked to my car and hopped in. I blasted the music and drove to Greenport to The Bartlett House. I only been there once, but I knew exactly how to get there. It took me a little over 2 hours to get into Greenport this time. I parked three blocks down the street. It was about 4pm when I reached the beach that The Bartlett House faced. I watched as people set up speakers on a stage, they placed a wooden dance floor right over the sand, and canopies of light hanging from wooden posts. It looked like they were having a party on the beach.

I started walking closer to The Bartlett House. I stood at the back near the opened veranda doors and it was just my luck to hear Charlie's laugh and then Tommy's voice. It took a lot out of me to walk away from her laugh. I walked along the beach.

Why was I here? What was I trying to find out? That she was in love with someone else and not me? I think I already figured that out. There was a playground a short walk up the beach. I sat on the swing and watched as the last phases of the party were set up. From there I could see everything. I watched as people started to make their way across the beach to the dance floor. The band started playing country songs. Ones that I never recognized and then the one that I did recognized blared out of the speakers. Charlie loved this song. I stood up and leaned against the poles that held up the swing set as I watched my Charlie walk hand in hand across the sand with Tommy. She was now pulling him on the dance floor laughing and glowing. Why didn't she ever look like that with me? Tommy twirled her on the dance floor and brought her close to him. I fought with myself not to run over there and claim my love for Charlie. Wouldn't I want her to be happy? I couldn't watch anymore when he placed a delicate kiss on her lips and the crowd started to clap and cheer for the man that stole my heart away. I walked away and held back the tears that were trying to break free. I loved Charlie and I'll do anything in my power to get her back.   She loves me. She just forgot that she does.

I drove back to Charlie's house parked my car on the corner and let myself in. I set my phone alarm for early in the morning. I wanted to be up to greet Charlie when she came home. I crawled into Charlie's bed and took a deep breath to take in her sweet strawberry and cream shampoo, that still was on her pillow.

I woke up the next morning and sat back at the kitchen table. I finally heard a car pull into the driveway and the front door opened.

"Finally you're home."

I stood up

"What are you doing here?"

"Charlie, the lying has gone too far."

"What lying? I broke up with you because your lying had gone to far."

"Why? Why did you break up with me? Charlie we were doing fine. Please. I need you now," I whispered.

"Jay, you know my sister told me everything about what my mom did and I think it was wrong for her to do that to you. You broke up with me for a reason. A reason that might have been our destiny.   My mom tried to change something that wasn't meant to be. I was meant to have Tommy's baby and be with him."

I was getting annoyed.   That's not the answer I wanted to here.

"Are you done with your speech?"

"Yes, I am." She walked toward me. "You knew things had gotten strange between us. I just couldn't fall in love with you the way it was before you left me. I don't want to force you to stay with me and become a father to a child that isn't even yours. It's not fair to you or me."

I walked away from her. I hated what she was saying to me. This is not how it was supposed to go. She was supposed to choose me not him.

"Please let's not make a big deal out of this and let's just end it," Charlie said calmly.

I couldn't take it anymore. My head started to hurt really bad. I went right into her face and started to yell. "You're the most irritating and confusing person I've ever been with!" I grabbed her shoulders and shook her. I didn't care if her head fell right off her shoulders.

"Get your hands off her," I vaguely heard Tommy shout from the doorway of the apartment.

I turned around. Everything felt like it was in slow motion. "Who are you to tell me what to do?" I shouted right into his face. "I asked you a question. Answer me!"

This man was looking at me with the coldest eyes I've ever seen. "I think Charlie has told you how she feels. I think you should just listen to her and leave."

"Honestly man, you can have her. She's a complete whore anyway." I started to walk toward the door. "I think it was you," pointing at Tommy. "You turned her into a whore. When she was with me she was not the way she is now."

Before I could step out of the way Tommy hit me with so much force that I fell right through the screen door.

"Don't ever call her names like that. Get out of here! I don't want to ever see you back around this house."

I stood up and dusted off my pants. It didn't even faze me that I just was pushed through a door. I was determined to approach Mary. I was furious with her. She told me Charlie would choose me.

I walked up to the front of the house and stormed in to confront Mary. She was sitting in the kitchen with Annabel. I went into the kitchen and pushed Annabel out of my way. Annabel stumbled, but caught herself. I wanted to lose my mind on Mary. She was a selfish, inconsiderate, spoiled bitch. Mary stood up and walked to Annabel.

"Are you okay?" she asked Annabel.

"Oh, I'm sorry if I pushed your precious daughter out of my way. I wanted to get to you."

"Jay, we can talk about this like civilized adults." She started to back away from me. I liked how scared she was of me.

"It was okay when it was about you. It was okay when you needed me to help *you,* but now that it's for me you want to *be civilized*. You don't care about me or your daughters. You're only concerned about your well-being."

I stopped talking when I heard the front door open and two small boys came running in. "Grandma, Grandma. We're here."

Mary took her grandchildren in her arms and hugged them tight. She kissed them both on their cheeks. Nina and Albert walked in afterwards.

"Hey, Mom," she called from the door.

"Jay, we can talk about this some other time. My family is here now. Please leave and I'll give you a call."

She walked to the back door and opened it for me.

"Sorry for pushing you Annabel," I said sincerely.

I walked out and stopped by the bushes were the opened window was. I squatted behind the bushes and sat there. I heard Annabel walked into the room with Mary. I peeked over the window sill so I could see them.

"What was his problem?" Annabel asked.

"Jay? Nothing. He's just annoyed that Charlie is back with Tommy. That's it."

How would you know she was back with him?" Nina asked as she walked into the kitchen.

"Oh. I don't know. I just assumed. I saw boxes in front of the garage and knew that Charlie kicked out Jay. I just assumed Tommy came back into the picture."

"Mom, I know you're lying," Annabel said. "Now tell us what really happened."

"Yeah, Mom. Why don't you tell Annabel what really happened?"

"Nina shut your big mouth. I'm surprised at you. Telling Charlie what I specifically told you not to tell her."

"Mom, please. Your crazy. You knew there was something mentally wrong with Jay. You said it all the time when Charlie was dating him. Dad always said he had it well controlled so it was never a threat to Charlie. How could you make a man that's mentally ill your go-getter? You should've just done it yourself. I think what you did was horrible. You should be ashamed to call yourself a mother."

They knew the whole time something was off about me. I thought I never allowed it to show. I was always very careful. There was only one time I lost it in the Romeo's house. Charlie went out with Marisa and came home late. I rang the doorbell one in the morning. Mary answered and said she wasn't home. All I did was take the pots of flowers they had on their stoop, and threw them as far as I could, while screaming at the top of my lungs. Mary could have called the cops. Instead, she called my parents to come and take me home. I jumped when I heard Annabel starting to yell.

"What did you do mom," Annabel yelled. "Why are you so psycho? How dare you get involved in someone else's life. If you ever do that to me I will never speak to you again," she yelled at the top of her lungs.

I'm surprised Charlie didn't hear them screaming.

"Forget both of you. I'm going upstairs to lay down. Thanks to both of you I have a splitting headache."

I watched as Mary left and Mel, Charlie's father came up from the basement. What was he doing chit-chatting with Tommy in the basement as Charlie cried because she was so upset that Tommy pushed me? What a pathetic little loser! It was time for me to leave before I got caught. I quietly snuck out of the bushes and through the neighbors yard. I didn't want to leave through the front of the house in fear of getting caught. I jogged around the corner to my Mustang, hopped in, turned the key in the ignition, and blasted the music. I drove aimlessly around Dobbs Ferry, the small two mile long town. I passed the church and the diner. I turned down Main Street, passed the pizzeria, and the Italian cafe that my mom and dad used to always take me to. I remember it like it was yesterday. I would order eggplant rolls to start and then get an order of penne vodka with a side of meatballs. My parents were always so amazed that I would eat the whole plate. Unfortunately, they never understood the side effects of my medication that I took. It would make my appetite insatiable. It was like I couldn't stop eating. I was very athletic so it never affected me.

I pulled up to the train station. I parked my car in the first spot. I went into my glove compartment and pulled out my bottle of vodka. I looked at the bottle. This is what makes me go on. I could hear the teenagers laughing and talking on the other side of the parking lot. That used to me and my friends. Now everyone has grown up. Their laughter was making my insides feel uncomfortable. I got out of the car and sat on the bench facing the train tracks. I knew the train schedule by heart. It's been the same since I used to take the train out to the city. I stood up slowly, and walked to the edge. My friends and I used to dodge the train. We would time it perfectly so none of us ever got hurt. One time Lenny, my best friend from school was super close. He rolled onto the other track just in time. It was a rush of adrenaline that every teenager needs.

I walked over to the train schedule to make sure I had the time right and I did. The next train was due in five minutes from now. I put my hands in my pocket and paced until I felt the platform shake a little, the whistle from the train was in the distance, but close enough. I felt the adrenaline building up inside of me. I put an ear to ear grin on my face when I started to see the train in the distance. Maybe this time I won't dodge it. What do I have to live for anymore? I sat on the edge of the platform and dangled my feet over the edge. I place my hands behind me on the floor and pushed off the ground. I was on the tracks. I watched as the train came closer and closer. I could see the conductor's face through the glass yelling for me to move. I had nothing to live for anymore.

~

At the last second I dodged the train. I saw the conductor stick his face out the window and wave his fist in the air. I was such a wuss. I had nothing to live for and I couldn't even take my own life. I'm a complete loser! What now? I grabbed my vodka bottle from the side of the tracks, opened it, and took a quick gulp. I wiped off the drizzle that came down the side of my mouth. I sat on the tracks. I knew the next train wouldn't come for another hour. Maybe I'll try then.

I rolled off the tracks and lifted myself up on the platform. I watched as the teenagers drove their fancy cars to the end of the river to hang out. I walked off the platform and started heading to the end of the river. I saw the Santo twins and the beautiful Lindsey. All the teenage boys wanted Lindsey. She was only four years younger than me. I walked over to the twins and slapped both their hands.

"Hey, Jay. What brings you down to the river?" The better looking of the twins asked.

I ignored his question and gazed at Lindsey. She was beautiful with her long jet black hair and blue eyes. Her lips were juicy and plump. They were just waiting for me to kiss. I shook my head to get myself out of my daze. Lindsey known my family since she was 12. What was I thinking?

I looked at the Santo twins and slapped their hands, "I'll see you boys around."

The walk to my car seemed a lot longer than the walk to the end of the parking lot. I took my keys out of my pocket when I heard footsteps behind me. I didn't have to turn around to see who it was. I could smell her lilac perfume from a mile away.

"Where are you going?" she asked.

"I'm just taking a ride. Do you want to come?"

"I would like that."

I went around to the passenger side of the car and opened the door for her like the gentleman I always was. She hopped right in without a second thought. Why should she think twice? It was sweet Jay taking her for a ride. I drove around for a little while.

"So, Lindsey. How old are you now?"

"I just turned 18 last week."

"What are you doing hanging out at the river? Let's go and celebrate."

I drove up to the golf course and put my car in park.

"It's very dark up here," she said.

"Yup." That was all I could say.

"How are things going with Charlie?"

"Charlie who?"

"So you guys aren't a couple anymore?"

"Nope. She left me."

I watched in confusion as Lindsey climbed over the center console and straddled me in my seat. It happened so fast. She was kissing me hard. At first I started to push her away and then I started getting that anxious feeling. I pulled at her hair so hard that she yelled out. I ripped off the four buttons on her pink shirt that were holding her huge breast in place. I pushed my hand in her shirt and forcefully pulled one out. I pushed her back a little as she smiled.

"I didn't know you were so rough," she said breathlessly

"You don't know anything about me."

"What did you say?"

I could hear the fear in her voice. I didn't even recognize my own voice anymore. I ripped off the rest of her shirt and kissed and bit her down her neck so hard that I left welts all over her neck and breast.

"Jay, you're hurting me."

"Isn't this what you wanted?"

She started to say something but the force of my lips on hers stopped her.

"Jay. Please stop."

I felt her digging in her pants. Oh good. She was cooperating nicely.

Next thing I knew, Lindsey started to yell. "Help me! Help me!"

I pushed her off of me and saw her phone on the floor with the numbers 9-1-1 on the screen. I quickly stepped on the phone and crushed it it to pieces. I opened the door and stepped out of the car. She went to open the passenger side door. I grabbed her by her black long hair and pulled her out through the driver's side door. I threw her on the ground, got into my car, and speed off.

I was speeding all the way to the corner of Charlie's block and sat there. I pushed my seat all the way back and laid there. What was wrong with me? What did I just do?

~

I woke up the next morning with the sun beating in through my windshield. I squinted my eyes and put down the visor. I had a perfect view of Charlie's house. I looked at my watch and it was 7:30 in the morning. I sat in my car and focused on Charlie's house for over an hour. I was starting to get restless and decided to leave. I was just about to pull away when I saw Tommy walk out the door. He jumped into his Porsche and drove off. I gave him a few minutes and then followed him. I turned onto a street that was all too familiar to me. He stopped in front of Marisa's house. Detective Marshall answered the door and let Tommy right in. I wanted to go in and see what they were talking about, but I knew that was impossible. I decided to drive back to Charlie's house. I pulled up to the corner just in time to see her waddle out of her house and make her way down the block toward the hospital. She must of had a doctor's appointment. When she was completely out of sight I parked my car and went into her house. The door wasn't locked. What was the sense of changing locks when she never locked the door? I went into her room and found the musky smell of Tommy. I could feel myself going insane every minute that passed. I put on the water and decided to take a cold shower. I knew Tommy or Charlie could walk in any minute. I didn't care. I came out of the shower, brushed my teeth with Charlie's toothbrush, decide to stick Tommy's in the toilet, and put it back. I hated this man. He stole my life away from me and I was going to get it back in any way possible. When I was done acting like a little kid I walked back to my car and took out my bottle of vodka. It was three quarters full. I chugged it. It gave me just the buzz I needed. About 15 minutes passed when I walked back to Charlie's house and sat at the kitchen table. I heard the shower running. I didn't see anyone go into the house. I was either waiting for Charlie or Tommy and I didn't care who.

"Tommy is that you?" I heard Charlie call out. "Hello!"

I watched as Charlie came out of the bathroom and into the kitchen. I gave her a little wave as her eyes became wide.

"Umm, what are you doing here?"

"I think I live here," I said.

"Jay, I moved your stuff out a while ago."

"No, Charlie, you forced me to leave. I didn't want to leave. I had just started getting comfortable with my new life. I was going to become a father. I was doing well in school and as you already know, I didn't have to pay for a damn penny for law school."

I stood up from the table and let the chair slam on the floor. I walked toward her and I saw her face turn ghost-white. She shook a little and I could see her forehead start to glisten with sweat. She started to back up as far against the wall as she could go.

"While I was out trying to make a better life for us you were busy sneaking around with another man. What kind of person are you? Charlie."

"Jay, I didn't mean to hurt you." I could hear her voice getting shaky. "It was over between us a long time ago. We both know why you came back to be with me so don't lie to me or yourself about it."

I didn't want to hurt Charlie. I loved her. It was Tommy I wanted to hurt.

"Where is he?" I shouted.

"Who?" she whispered.

I can't believe what a liar she was turning out to be. Is she really going to make it like she doesn't know who I was asking for?

"Charlie, Charlie." I couldn't help the laughter that escaped my mouth. I poked her in her chest. "You know exactly who I'm talking about."

"Jay, stop. That hurts."

"Well, deal with it. You've been sneaking around for the last eight months with this creep. You always had some kind of excuse like "girls night out" or "going out with Marisa." You didn't think I knew who was driving that yellow Porsche. You lied and said it was Detective Marshall's car. What kind of person have you become?"

I was never this mad at Charlie. I could tell I was scaring her and I think I might have liked it.

"Jay, you didn't want to be with me. My mom paid you to stay with me. Why are you so upset about all of this? You left me, Jay. Remember you left me. I didn't leave you. I cared about you."

"Oh, did you care about me so much that you would sleep with the first guy you met? I knew you would turn into a slut."

I was screaming and I didn't care. I watched as she put her hands over her ears.

"You were always such a baby. Oh, I'm sorry, is my voice scaring you? Poor, poor Charlie."

I went to say more but she was walking across the room toward the bedroom. I tried to grab her shirt. I felt like I was moving in slow motion. When I moved my hand to grab her I saw a rainbow of colors. I looked around and everything had a rainbow tint. I jumped when she slammed the bedroom door. I heard her fumbling with the knob to lock it. Did she really think the lock was going to keep me out? I started kicking the door.

"Come out, Charlie," I whispered. "Do you really think I would hurt you? What kind of man do you think I am? I was just really mad you chose him over me." I banged on the door. "Come on, Charlie, baby. Come out and talk to me."

I watched as she opened the door slowly and then the headache hit me hard. I was seeing double and the rainbow of colors was completely blocking my vision. I slid down the wall holding my head. I could smell her strawberries and cream shampoo as she bent down to comfort me. I grabbed the top of her arm and dragged her to me. I pulled her closer to me and started kissing her cheek.

"Charlie, we could have been so good together. Why did you have to ruin it?" Are you speechless?"

I twisted her head so she was facing me. I grabbed her shoulder and pushed her to the floor. The pain in my head was unreal. I will get through it. I laid my body over hers. I started pushing down her pajama bottoms.

Jay, please! You're hurting me!" she said through labored breaths.

"I'm not hurting you. I would never hurt you."

I started biting her lips and kissing her hard.

"Jay...please...stop! You're hurting me," she cried.

I watched as she wiped off my kiss. There was blood all over her hand. It didn't faze me.

"Just like you to wipe my kiss right off your mouth. I don't care if you're not allowed to have sex while you're pregnant. You're going to have sex right now," I yelled.

"Jay please. Stop. Please," she shouted. "We can talk about this."

"I'm sure you don't tell...what's-his-name? Tommy Rhodes to stop. Do you like it when he is rough with you?"

She tried to push me off of her. Every time she would push on my chest my arm would automatically push her back down. I ripped off her pajama bottoms completely and looked at her swollen belly and then stopped. What was I doing? I can't do this to her. I love her. I went to roll away from her when I was pulled off of her and smashed in the face. I was thrown outside before I could shake the dizzy feeling off.   I was on the floor searching for something, anything that could help me defend myself.   I grabbed a sharp rock as Tommy lunged toward me. I stuck the sharp rock into his arm and pulled it down. When he pulled away from me I saw his blood all over my hand. If only I got it in his heart I wouldn't have to deal with him anymore. I tried to stand up. I was back on my knees before I could even lift my head. I saw red sirens in the distance. I looked to see if Tommy was on the ground anywhere. He was gone. He had disappeared.

~

I woke up to a man handcuffing me saying, "You have the right to remain silent anything you say will......"   I stopped listening after that.   I was helped to my feet and when I was standing at my full 6'2 height, I put my head down in shame.   I was in Charlie's driveway with blood all over my hands. Did I kill her?

Officer Gates is short, and robust. He had a full head of black hair and beady brown eyes. He walked me up to the Dobbs Ferry police car, stood on his tip-toes, placed his hand on my head, and ducked me into the car. I watched as all of Charlie's neighbors surrounded her driveway. All the families that I knew for so long watched as I was put into the police car like I was a criminal. It took five minutes to get to the police station. I was taken out of the car with Officer Gates holding me by the handcuffs. He placed me in a holding cell. I heard him talk to the other officer, I forgot his name.

"That's the Bushnell boy. Give his father a call. At least he has a lawyer in the family. Poor kid was studying to be a lawyer himself. I don't know what the hell came over him. Clean record until an hour ago."

I didn't know what else to do. I crawled up into a ball and cried myself to sleep. I was awoken by the jail gates being opened. I peeked opened my eye to see my father standing in front of me.

"Come on Officer Gates, you couldn't even let him wash his hands."

I looked at my hands. They were now covered with dry blood.

"It's not my job to baby the inmates."

"*Inmate*? Is that what you call a boy you knew his whole life? *An inmate*? Did you find Tommy? He's the one you should be questioning."

"He's in the hospital getting his arm stitched up."

My dad sat next to me on the bench. I just looked at him and started crying. "I'm sorry, Dad. Please forgive me. I didn't mean to kill her. I didn't want her to leave me. Dad I love her."

"Son, slow down. You didn't kill Charlie. We don't know the outcome of the babies yet. We are waiting on the report from the hospital."

I took a deep breath. "What do you mean babies?"

"Half of the report came in from the doctors into the police station. She was pregnant with twins. She's in the delivery room in the hospital right now," Officer Gates said.

I sat with my head in my hands. "I have a very bad headache and I need my pills. I don't even remember what happened."

"I know.   Let me see if I can get you some pain medication. I will call the pharmacist to verify that you're on a medication to control your bipolar disorder."

"I guess I shouldn't have gone off the pills."

"It's okay. We'll figure it all out."

I waited for the next two hours. I paced, I sat, I stood, and I even leaned on the jail bars. My head was killing me and I needed my pills. I knew it was a little too late to want my pills on an everyday basis. They always say something drastic has to happen in order for you to want to do the right thing.

I finally heard someone approaching the jail cell.   I heard Officer Gates and my dad talking, "Yes, one of them died. Charlie is doing fine. She's a little shook up and her mother refused to let me see her to ask her what happened. I'm going to go in now and talk to Jay. Hopefully, he can explain to me exactly what happened."

Officer Gates opened the cell for my dad to come in. He closed the cell immediately like I was a murderer.

My dad sat on the bench so I followed his lead. "Jay, can you remember anything that happened?"

I just shook my head no. It wasn't even a blur. It was like I was missing a complete day of my life.

"Are you aware that Lindsey called the police about an hour before the police picked you up from Charlie's house?"

"No. I wasn't aware."

"Did you do anything to Lindsey?"

I put my head in my hands. "I was at the river and I was going for a ride. She hopped in my car and we drove up to the country club. That's all I remember."

I watched as my Dad wrote word for word of what I said.

"When was the last time you took your medication?"

"I'm not sure."

"We are waiting for the doctor's report to see if it can help you in defense of your charges."

"What are my charges?"

"Murder!"

"What? Who did I kill?"

"One of Charlie's unborn babies."

"Come on Dad. That can't be right. The baby wasn't even born yet. It wasn't like I wanted to kill the baby."

"If Tommy didn't come in and get you off Charlie, you would have killed her too."

"No, Dad. I wouldn't have killed her. I love her."

"We are hoping with your illness we can get it reduced to attempted rape, resisting arrest, and assaulting a police officer. It all depends on when the last time you took your medicine was. We are due in court tomorrow morning." My dad stood up. "Rest for tonight."

I hugged my dad and watched him leave.

Rest. How did he want me to rest? I murdered someone. Why didn't I just take my medicine? What did I do? I just ruined my whole life in one day. I could feel my eyes welling up with tears and then they just started pouring out.

"Charlie, Charlie!" I yelled.

I pounded the bench and threw it across the room. I shook the bars, screaming at the top of my lungs until Officer Gates came in, restrained me, and placed the handcuffs back on me.

~

"Why is he back in handcuffs?" I vaguely heard my dad's voice. The door to my cell opened and my dad was sitting me up. He looked at the bench across the room. "Please, take these off him."

Officer Gates came in and took the handcuffs off. I rubbed my wrists.

"Here is a suit, and clean underwear. Your mom packed a toothbrush and deodorant."

"Mommy knows? You told Mom?"

"Come on Jay. What did you want me to say?"

I put my head down. "Did the doctor call?"

"Yes, before court you can take your medication."

For the first time ever in my life I was excited I needed medication to control my behavior.

My dad left. I got dressed, brushed my teeth, and took a long hard look in the mirror. Looking back was a person I never saw before.

My dad came back 20 minutes later with my bottle of medication.

"The judge said you can take this, but first they have to do blood work."

About five minutes later a lady that held a brief case walked into the cell.

"Oh good you made it. Jay, this is Nurse Tucker. She needs to draw one vial of blood and then you can take your medication."

She opened up her briefcase and took out a retractable needle, a blue elastic band, and a band-aide. I held out my arm so Nurse Tucker could take my blood. She tied the elastic band around my arm and pushed on my arm to find a vein. I was waiting for her to tell me this was only going to pinch a little like when I was a kid, but she said nothing. She took my blood, labeled the vial, and placed it back in the suitcase.

"The results should be ready by the time you get to court," she said.

"Thank you," my dad said.

My dad handed me my pills. I shook two out of the bottle and swallowed them. I needed them so badly I didn't even need water with them.

"Why did they need blood?"

"They need to make sure you haven't taken your medication. Since you haven't taken them in a while we can get your charge reduced."

I walked out of the cell still handcuffed. They couldn't take me out of my handcuffs until we were in court. Obviously, my dad didn't know I had a stash of pills in my closet under the floor. I knew the test was going to come out positive. I already knew I was in jail for murder. I wanted them to just take me now, but I wanted my dad to feel that at least he tried to do something.

I walked into the court room. The court officer removed my handcuffs. I looked at the audience. The only people I recognized was my mom, my brother, James who was six years older then me, and my best friend from school, Lenny. We lost touch when he went to college in California. We spoke on the phone for the first six months. I even went out to see him in California for week. I remember having a great time.

I saw a reporter sitting in the way back with his pad and paper on his lap ready to hear the case. I looked a few rows up and saw two law students sitting there. I knew they were law students because they had binders on their laps getting ready to take notes.

Who was I expecting to come and watch me go to jail for life? Charlie, holding just one of her babies? Or maybe Tommy.

"Where's Charlie?" I asked.

"Jay, she's at her son's funeral as we speak. Give me one good reason why you would ask for her?"

I just looked down. Why was I asking for her? I was dead in her mind. I sat at the table with my dad's partner, Alex. He would be defending me. My dad sat with my mom. He placed his arm around her as she dabbed her eyes with a tissue. She looked up and I looked down. I couldn't look at her. What a disappointment I am.

The judge walked in, "All rise."

I stood up. The nurse that took my blood walked up to the stand as soon as we all sat.

"These are the results for Jason Bushnell's blood work showing whether or not he was medicated at the time of the attack. Jay is a man living with a bipolar disorder that was kept under control. If he had taken his medication then the case will be continued. If he didn't it will be dismissed because he is a man with a mental disability and charges will be lowered," The District Attorney said.

The judge opened the envelope. It was like the court room was in slow motion. He read the results and slammed his hammer on the table.

"Jason Bushnell is on trial for attempted rape, resisting arrest, assaulting a police officer and murder of

Charlotte Romeo's son." My dad jumped up. I signaled for him to sit down. "Jason how do you plead?"

"Guilty."

The judge slammed the hammer down on the table. "You are being charged with assaulting a police officer, murder of an unborn child, resisting arrest, and attempted rape. I'm sentencing you to 15-25 years in the state penitentiary. This court is dismissed."

I closed my eyes and put my head down. The court officer came over and placed the handcuffs back on my wrists. I could hear my mom's sobs and my dad trying to console her with his whispering. I heard the reporter make his last mark on the paper and exit the court room. The law students gasped when I made my plea. The court officer walked me through the doors of the court room. We walked out and into the car that would be bringing me to my new home. Countless memories flooded my mind. They started with when I first met Charlie, her laugh and how she rambled. My mom sitting at the island in the kitchen reading her romance stories, my dad laughing his hearty laugh, and his faith in me to the very end.

If you love *The Proposition* you will fall in love with *Cuff Links and Hair Pins*.

There are a few things twenty-one year old Charlotte Romeo was sure she'd never do: She'd never have a one-night stand; never get pregnant before she was married; and never bury a loved one unexpectedly.

Now Charlotte Romeo's longtime boyfriend jars her perfect world by leaving her. Her best friend persuades her to have a one-night stand. A few weeks later she gets food poisoning that she can't seem to get rid of. A trip to the doctors confirms she's pregnant.

She searches and finds her mysterious one-night stand, with the help of her two sisters and best friend. When Charlotte's ex-boyfriend comes barreling back into her life as unexpectedly as he left, her mysterious man vanishes. Just as everything seems to be settling in, Charlotte gets an unexpected visitor that will change her life forever.

She will soon discover that her unexpected visitor has many secrets that will lead Charlotte on a path to either help him or leave him. In the next thirty-six weeks, Charlotte will learn how to love, learn what family really means and mourn a death that a twenty-one year old shouldn't have to deal with.

Get your copy today on amazon

About the Author

Marianna Albert is the author of Cuff Links and Hair Pins. She has a B.S. in Behavioral Science and an M.S. in Education from Mercy College. She worked as a special education teacher for five years and lives in Dobbs Ferry, New York with her husband and four children.

www.readawaywithmarianna.com

Marianna Albert